I0439986

Marine Air Traffic Control Detachment Handbook

U.S. Marine Corps

ISTRIBUTION STATEMENT A: Approved for public release; distribution is unlimited.

PCN: 143 000030 00

To Our Readers

Changes: Readers of this publication are encouraged to submit suggestions and changes that will improve it. Recommendations may be sent directly to Commanding General, Marine Corps Combat Development Command, Doctrine Division (C 42), 3300 Russell Road, Suite 318A, Quantico, VA 22134-5021 or by fax to 703-784-2917 (DSN 278-2917) or by E-mail to **nancy.morgan@usmc.mil**. Recommendations should include the following information:

- Location of change
  Publication number and title
  Current page number
  Paragraph number (if applicable)
  Line number
  Figure or table number (if applicable)
- Nature of change
  Add, delete
  Proposed new text, preferably double-
  spaced and typewritten
- Justification and/or source of change

Additional copies: A printed copy of this publication may be obtained from Marine Corps Logistics Base, Albany, GA 31704-5001, by following the instructions in MCBul 5600, *Marine Corps Doctrinal Publications Status.* An electronic copy may be obtained from the Doctrine Division, MCCDC, world wide web home page which is found at the following universal reference locator: **https://www.doctrine.usmc.mil**.

Unless otherwise stated, whenever the masculine gender is used, both men and women are included.

DEPARTMENT OF THE NAVY
Headquarters United States Marine Corps
Washington, DC 20380-1775

11 November 2004

FOREWORD

The Marine air command and control system (MACCS) provides the Marine aviation combat element commander with the means to exercise control of those organic and nonorganic aviation assets that are necessary to support Marine air-ground task force (MAGTF) operations. Marine Corps Warfighting Publication (MCWP) 3-25, *Control of Aircraft and Missiles,* addresses basic planning considerations for MACCS operations, employment, and interoperability among MACCS and joint Service agencies.

MCWP 3-25.8, *Marine Air Traffic Control Detachment Handbook*, complements and expands on the information in MCWP 3-25 by focusing on the details of Marine air traffic control detachment (MATCD) operations and the role it plays in MAGTF, joint, and multinational operations. Intended for MAGTF, naval expeditionary force, and joint force commanders and staffs, MCWP 3-25.8 highlights MATCD—

- Organization.
- Equipment.
- Planning considerations.
- Operational fundamentals.
- Employment options.

By investigating these areas, MCWP 3-25.8 provides the requisite information needed by commanders and staffs to understand and evaluate the operational principles and capabilities of various MATCD employment options.

Supersession: MCWP 3-25.8, *Marine Air Traffic Control Detachment Handbook*, dated 1 August 1997.

Reviewed and approved this date.

BY DIRECTION OF THE COMMANDANT OF THE MARINE CORPS

J. N. MATTIS
Lieutenant General, U.S. Marine Corps
Commanding General
Marine Corps Combat Development Command

Publication Control Number: 143 000030 00

DISTRIBUTION STATEMENT A: Approved for public release; distribution is unlimited.

Marine Air Traffic Control Detachment Handbook

Table of Contents

Chapter 1. Fundamentals

Chapter 2. System Description

Chapter 4. Operations

Appendices

Figures

Tables

CHAPTER 1
FUNDAMENTALS

MISSION

The mission of Marine air traffic control (ATC) is to provide all-weather radar/nonradar approach, departure, en route, and tower ATC services to friendly aircraft.

MATCD is the principal terminal ATC organization within MACCS. Three MATCDs are structured to operate as subordinate elements of Marine air control squadron (MACS). MATCD normally deploys as a part of MACCS within MAGTF, but may also deploy independently or as part of a joint force should the mission dictate.

Each MATCD is organized and equipped to provide continuous all-weather ATC services to an independent and geographically separated main air base or air facility, and two remote air sites or points. Appendix A describes these forward operating bases (FOBs).

MATCD also functions as an integral part of a MAGTF or joint force integrated air defense system (IADS). Marine ATC equipment is maintained by MATCD and is supported by Naval Air Systems Command (NAVAIR).

RESPONSIBILITIES

- Provides airspace control, management, and surveillance for its designated airspace sector.

- Provides required ATC services to support MAGTF and joint operations.

- Provides navigational assistance to friendly aircraft, including en route ATC services.

- Interfaces with the MACCS, other military command and control (C2) agencies, and/or civilian agencies/organizations to include the Federal Aviation Administration (FAA) and International Civil Aviation Organization (ICAO).

- Provides personnel to the survey, liaison, reconnaissance party team to ensure air traffic procedures, MATCD siting criteria, and terminal instrument procedures (TERPs) are considered and addressed during the site survey.

- Provides liaison personnel for the joint staff, ATC agencies, airspace management, C2, and host nation (HN) as required for integrated planning and management of air operations.

- Provides control tower, radar, and nonradar approach/departure control services within its assigned airspace.

- Provides precision and nonprecision navigational aids (NAVAIDS).

- Provides automatic landing system approach and landing services under all-weather landing conditions.

- Displays and disseminates appropriate air and ground situation information to designated higher and adjacent air C2 agencies, including the Marine tactical air command center (TACC), tactical air operations center (TAOC), early warning/control, direct air support center (DASC), air defense detachment, and low altitude air defense (LAAD) battalion, while functioning as an integral element of the MACCS and/or joint force.

- Provides radar air surveillance data to the MAGTF/joint force via tactical digital information link (TADIL) B.

- Serves as the operational liaison between the MAGTF/joint force and national/international ATC agencies.

- Coordinates the activation and execution of the airfield base defense zone (BDZ).

- Provides ATC subject matter experts for essential liaison billets with the joint/multinational force and civil/military ATC agencies.

ORGANIZATION

MATCD's assigned mission and supporting task organization will determine the ATC element's exact crew requirements.

MATCD is led by a detachment commander who coordinates detachment activities and supervises the detachment's ATC watch officers. Watch officers are crew managers. MATCD crews are typically organized into command, radar control, tower control, and maintenance sections. Each detachment is organized to provide the MAGTF with two Marine air traffic control mobile teams (MMTs). Figure 1-1 on page 1-4 shows an MATCD's notional organization.

Command Section

The command section supervises and coordinates each MATCD's activities. The command section includes the operations officer/chief, detachment commander, noncommissioned officer in charge (NCOIC), tower chief, radar chief, maintenance officer, and the ATC watch commander.

There may be more than one ATC watch commander based on mission requirements. The number of crews required will dictate the controller structure.

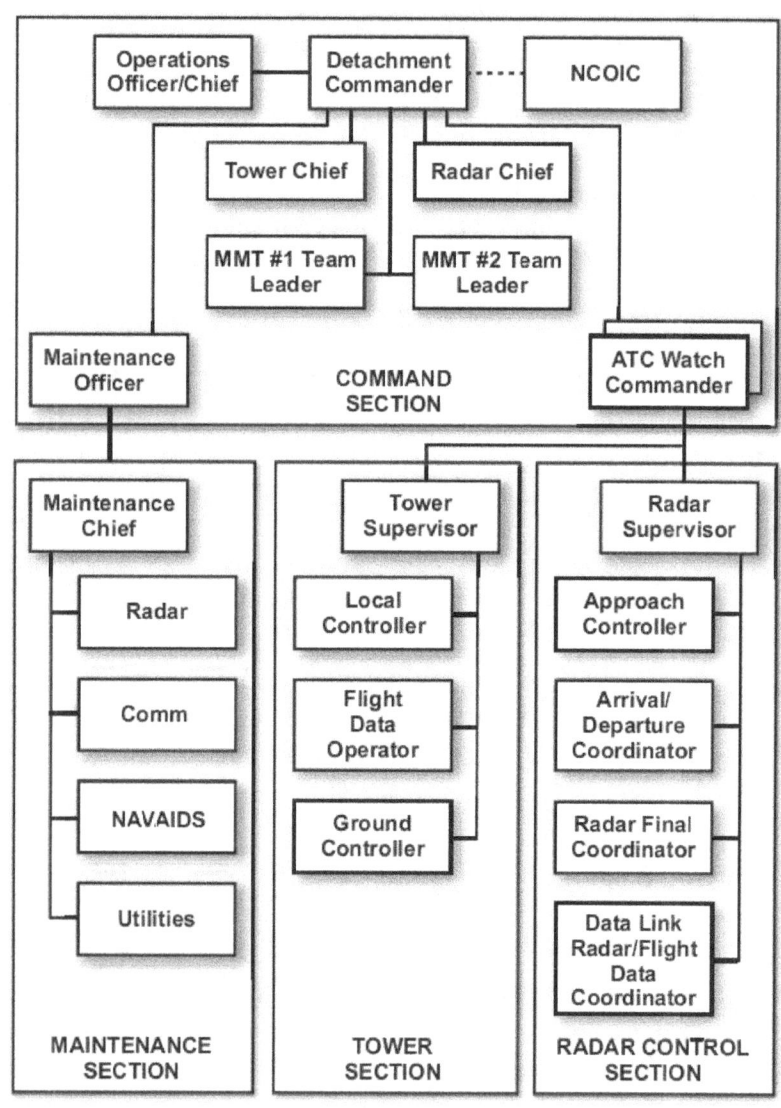

Figure 1-1. Notional MATCD Operational Organization.

Notes:
*There may be more than one ATC Watch Commander based on
 mission requirements.
*The number of crews required will dictate the controller structure.

Detachment Commander

The detachment commander is a military occupational specialty (MOS) 7220 ATC officer responsible for the ATC detachment command and its integration with the MACCS or joint agencies. Normally a captain, the detachment commander supervises the technical and tactical employment of the detachment personnel and equipment.

Noncommissioned Officer in Charge

The NCOIC is an MOS 7291/7257 air traffic controller. Normally a master sergeant, the NCOIC provides assistance and recommendations to the detachment commander concerning all aspects of operations, personnel, and administration.

Operations Officer/Chief

The operations officer/chief is an experienced MOS 7220/7291/ 7257 air traffic controller responsible for the detailed planning and coordination of training exercises and combat operations. ATC operations often require in-depth study and analysis of the required mission during the planning and predeployment process to ensure the proper personnel and equipment are deployed. Most deployments require detailed planning of the required ATC and airfield operations necessary for mission accomplishment. The ATC operations officer/chief ensures this coordination and planning is accomplished.

ATC Watch Commander

Responsibilities include—

- Detailed operation of the detachment's crew.
- Coordination between each of the detachment's sections.

- Coordination between the detachment, internal airfield units, and other MACCS agencies.

The watch officer billet is normally filled by either lieutenants or senior staff noncommissioned officers (SNCOs).

Maintenance Officer

Responsibilities include—

- Maintenance of all detachment ATC and combat equipment.
- Supervision and performance of the NAVAIDS, radar, communications, and auxiliary equipment sections.
- Timely logistical flow of necessary replacement parts and maintenance documentation.

Radar Chief

Responsibilities include—

- Planning and execution of the radar section and the coordination with outside agencies and other MACCS agencies as they relate to the radar section.
- Training, testing, and proficiency of all the radar section's controllers.
- Supervision of the radar crews to ensure continuity.

Tower Chief

Responsibilities include—

- Planning and execution of the tower section and the coordination with outside agencies and other MACCS agencies as they relate to the tower section.

- Training, testing, and proficiency of all the tower section's controllers.

- Supervising the tower crews to ensure continuity.

Maintenance Section

The maintenance section includes technicians from four specialty backgrounds required to maintain ATC equipment. The maintenance section contains radar, communications, NAVAIDS, and utilities technicians. The maintenance section is capable of repairing most equipment down to the microminiature component level and coordinating with the MALS to obtain replacement parts and logistical support.

Maintenance Chief

A MOS 5959 is responsible to the maintenance officer for the scheduling and performance of all maintenance management systems requirements and technical training within the four maintenance sections. He also coordinates all logistic support with S-6, S-4, and Marine aviation logistic squadrons.

Radar

Performs corrective and preventive maintenance for the AN/TPS-73, AN/TPN-22, AN/TSQ-131, and OA-9143/TSM-170 systems.

Communication

Performs corrective and preventive maintenance for the AN/TSQ-216, AN/TSQ-120B, AN/TSQ-131, and OA-9142/TSM-170 systems.

NAVAIDS

Performs corrective and preventive maintenance for the AN/TRN-44, AN/TRN-46, MEP531, and OA-9144/TSM-170 systems.

Utilities

Performs corrective and preventive maintenance for the MEP006A, HD-1099, and OA-9141/TSM-170 systems.

Tower Control Section

The tower control section is responsible for the control of friendly aircraft operating within the tower's assigned airspace. Airspace is typically limited to an area that can be visually observed and surveyed from the tower (approximately 5-nautical mile (nmi) radius from the airfield up to an altitude of 2,500-feet above ground level). The tower section is also responsible for air and vehicular traffic operating on runways, taxiways, and other designated areas of the airfield.

Tower Supervisor

Responsibilities include—

- Briefing the crew on the current tactical situation, weather, equipment, and airfield conditions.
- Coordinating and directing control of aircraft operating within the controlled airspace.
- Directing control of aircraft and surface vehicular traffic operating on runways, taxiways, and other designated movement areas of the airfield.

Local Controller

The local controller maintains visual surveillance of the controlled airspace and other movement areas to formulate and issue clearances and control instructions to aircraft operating under the jurisdiction of the tower. Clearances and control instructions given by the local controller provide necessary separation between aircraft.

Flight Data Operator

The flight data operator posts, relays, and coordinates aircraft movement data and posts weather updates.

Ground Controller

The ground controller provides general surveillance of the airfield and formulates and issues ground movement clearances to aircraft and vehicles operating on the airport movement area.

Radar Control Section

Under the cognizance of the radar supervisor, the radar control section manages assigned/designated airspace. The radar control section's division of responsibilities (figure 1-2, page 1-10) can be compared to a bull's eye (though not necessarily concentric) with the approach, arrival/departure, and final controllers each responsible for aircraft control within an assigned ring. The radar control section transmits information via data link or voice cross tell to other air control agencies, supervises MATCD execution of emission control (EMCON) conditions set by the TACC, and employs appropriate electronic protection (EP) measures. The radar section also integrates air traffic into the air defense system,

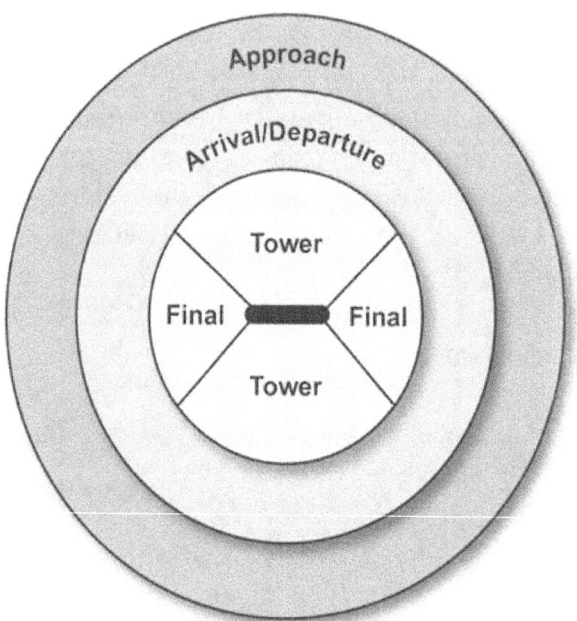

Figure 1-2. Radar Control Section Responsibilities.

coordinates the BDZ, and forwards radar surveillance via data link to other MAGTF/joint C2 agencies.

Approach Controller

Responsibilities include—

- Maintaining radar surveillance of approach control airspace.
- Providing ATC services to aircraft.
- Determining the separation/sequencing of aircraft and initiating/receiving radar handoffs from other control agencies.

- Processing and coordinating aircraft passing through the terminal control area (TCA) entering arrival/departure airspace.

While radar is the preferred method of separating aircraft, approach controllers can provide navigation and aircraft separation information using nonradar procedures.

Arrival/Departure Controller

The arrival/departure controller accepts radar or procedural handoffs from the approach controller and provides ATC services for aircraft until they reach approach minimums or are handed off to the final controller or tower controller. The arrival/departure controller may use radar or nonradar methods of control to process aircraft within the arrival/departure airspace.

Final Controller

The final controller conducts precision approaches using the automatic carrier landing system (ACLS) and radar approaches using the airport surveillance radar. The final controller typically provides these services to aircraft during periods of poor weather or visibility. Aircraft operating under visual flight rules (VFR) conditions typically contact the airfield tower to conduct a VFR approach.

Data Link Radar/Flight Data Coordinator

Responsibilities include—

- Orderly functioning of the data link with other MACCS/joint Service ATC agencies.

- Accuracy of situation displays, and track coordination functions with the data link's interface control unit.

- Radar flight data handling, processing clearances, and coordinating with the tower and external ATC agencies.

MARINE AIR TRAFFIC CONTROL MOBILE TEAM

The MMT is trained and equipped to provide initial rapid response ATC, and command, control, and communications (C3) to support MAGTF and joint missions. MMTs support operations at air sites, forward arming and refueling points (FARPs), rapid ground refueling (RGR) points or lagger points.

As a stand alone ATC capability, the MMT can task-organize to provide ATC services for airfield seizures, noncombatant evacuation operations (NEOs), domestic or foreign humanitarian assistance operations, civil assistance operations, and other short duration MAGTF/joint operations. Although often employed in conjunction with other combat units, the MMT provides all equipment to be self-sustained during initial operations.

Functions

The MMT rapidly establishes and controls tactical landing zones (TLZs), which are temporary austere landing strips for fixed-wing aircraft, and helicopter landing zones (HLZs) for rotary-wing aircraft in remote locations. The MMT is specifically trained and task-organized to—

- Provide ATC services at designated TLZs/HLZs including formulating ATC procedures, and issuing ATC clearances, instructions, and advisories to effect safe, orderly, and expeditious movement of air traffic in their assigned airspace.

- Establish a TCA around each TLZ and controlling all air traffic within this area under VFR and instrument flight rules conditions.

- Recommend/assist in TLZ/HLZ site selection. Determine each site's operational suitability for the number and type of aircraft.

- Conduct TLZ/HLZ and assault zone surveys. Surveys determine the suitability of the landing surface for operations, annotate hazards to aviation to include obstructions/obstacles, and provide operational data.

- Mark and light TLZs/HLZs for fixed-wing and rotary-wing aircraft.

- Provide terminal NAVAIDS and beacons.

- Develop terminal instrument procedures for TLZs/HLZs.

- Coordinate with civil and military control agencies.

- Provide air-ground and air to air communications to link austere sites with higher and adjacent C2 agencies.

- Provide limited weather observations and information.

- Only in extreme cases will MMT function without an air boss. Air boss is an aviator normally from the unit being supported.

- Provide positive control of personnel and equipment within the FOB, air site, air point, FARP, RGR, or lagger area.

MATCD is structured to provide personnel and equipment for two MMTs. One MMT utilizes the remote landing site tower (RLST) for its organic communications capability, and the other MMT utilizes man-portable radios. RLST's radios can be removed and operated in a man-pack configuration for foot-mobile operations.

CHAPTER 2
SYSTEM DESCRIPTION

The MATCD's equipment provides ATCs with the information necessary to maintain situational awareness and to effectively control and coordinate friendly aircraft activities in and around FOBs. MATCD equipment also provides information to aircraft navigating in MATCD controlled airspace. The MATCD task-organizes the equipment it needs to meet mission requirements.

MARINE AIR TRAFFIC CONTROL AND LANDING SYSTEM

The Marine air traffic control and landing system (MATCALS) provides continuous radar approach, departure, and en route ATC capabilities. MATCALS collects, evaluates, and displays air track data and disseminates information to other air control agencies. MATCALS consists of three subsystems: AN/TPS-73 ATC subsystem (ATCS), AN/TPN-22 all-weather landing system (ALS), and AN/TSQ-131 control and communications subsystem (CCS).

AN/TPS-73 Air Traffic Control Subsystem

The AN/TPS-73 ATCS (figure 2-1) is a two-dimensional, transportable, tactical airport surveillance radar system operating in the E band (2705 to 2895 megahertz [MHz]). This nonlinear radar is capable of a 60 nmi surveillance range for its primary radar and a 120-nmi search range for its secondary radar (identification, friend or foe [IFF]). It can also detect airborne targets up to an altitude of 60,000 feet. The AN/TPS-73 ATCS can interrogate IFF modes I, II, III, IV, and C. Radar and IFF information from the ATCS are processed within the CCS and can be forwarded to other agencies via data link (TADIL B) and/or voice communications. The AN/TPS-73 ATCS can simultaneously detect and track up to 600 air targets.

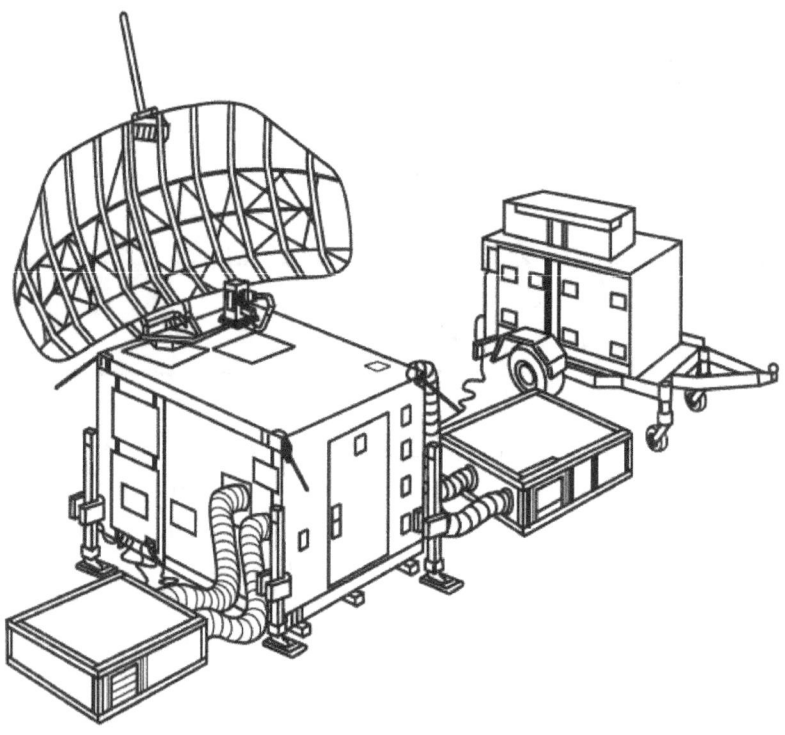

Figure 2-1. AN/TPS-73 Air Traffic Control Subsystem.

AN/TPN-22 All-Weather Landing System

The AN/TPN-22 ALS (figure 2-2) is an I band (9000-9200 mHz), three-dimensional, transportable phased array radar that provides the MATCD with tactical precision approach capabilities. The AN/TPN-22 ALS's pencil beam radar has a 10-nmi range and an 8-degree (-1 to +7 degree) angular coverage in elevation. The AN/TPN-22 ALS provides ACLS Mode I/IA, Mode II, and Mode III approach services via TADIL C for all-weather landings. The AN/TPN-22 ALS is capable of automatic tracking for up to six aircraft simultaneously.

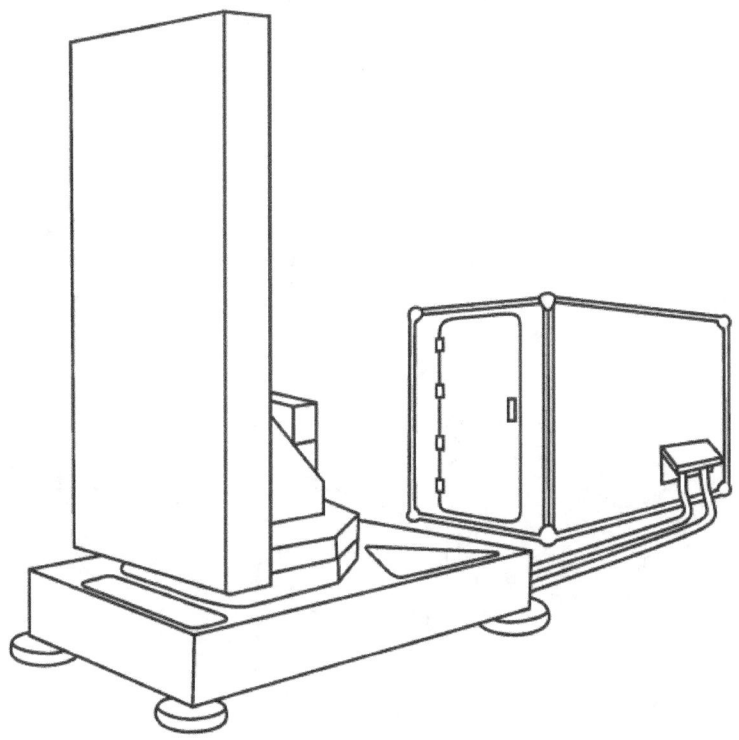

Figure 2-2. AN/TPN-22 All-Weather Landing System.

AN/TSQ-131 Control and Communications Subsystem

The AN/TSQ-131 CCS (figure 2-3) is the central interface for processing and displaying radar information, and performing as the
central communications platform for radar operations. It functions
as a collection point for radar data produced by the ATCS and ALS.
The CCS consists of two International Standards Organization
shelters that allow for its employment in either a single or dual
shelter configuration. Each shelter provides four processor display
system (PDS) consoles that serve as operational workstations for
crew members. Each PDS has its own communications capability.
In addition to intercommunications and switchboard circuits, the
CCS provides access to one high frequency (HF), three very high
frequency (VHF) amplitude modulation (AM), one VHF frequency

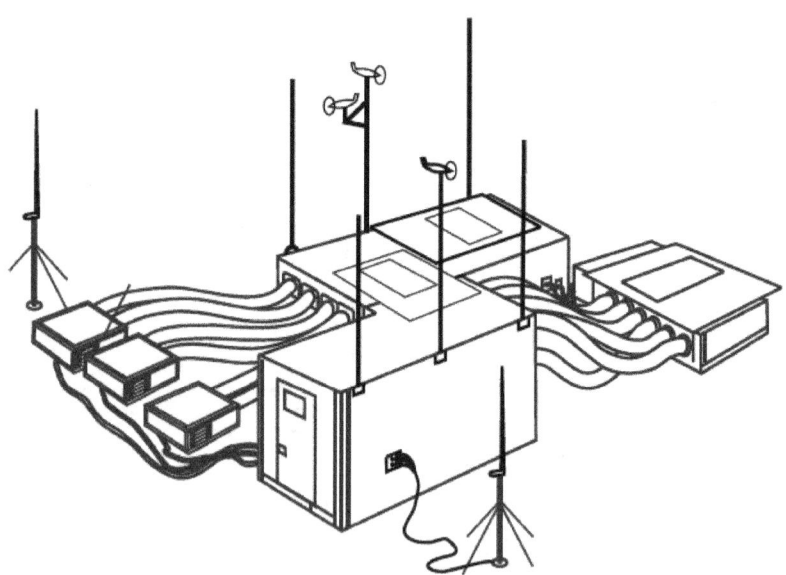

**Figure 2-3. AN/TSQ-131 Control and
Communications Subsystem.**

modulation (FM), six ultrahigh frequency (UHF) radios, and two FM/VHF/UHF radios with single-channel ground and airborne radio system (SINCGARS), HAVEQUICK, and satellite capability. One UHF radio is reserved for TADIL C. In addition to accessing single channel radios, the CCS provides access to 10 external telephone lines.

The CCS has the capability to automatically exchange certain elements of command tactical intelligence and situational data with other TADIL B capable units to include the TAOCs, other ATC detachments, and the TACC. The AN/TSQ-131 is also capable of encrypted communications.

OTHER AIR TRAFFIC CONTROL EQUIPMENT

AN/TSQ-120 A/B Air Traffic Control Central (ATC Tower)

The ATC tower (figure 2-4, page 2-6) is a transportable tower facility that provides operators with a 360-degree visual observance of aircraft, both on the ground and in the air, operating within a designated control zone and visual control over ground vehicles operating in the vicinity of the runway. The ATC tower can be erected to heights of 8, 16, or 24 feet. The ATC tower provides three operator positions from which aircraft and airfield control is effected through the use of radio communications and visual aids. The AN/TSQ-120A provides operators with access to one HF, three VHF/AM, one VHF/FM, five UHF radios, and up to 10 telephone lines. The AN/TSQ-120B provides operators with one HF, and eight VHF(AM and FM)/UHF radios that are SINGCARS and HAVEQUICK capable. All radio communications are recorded. Visual communication is effected through the use of an Aldis lamp.

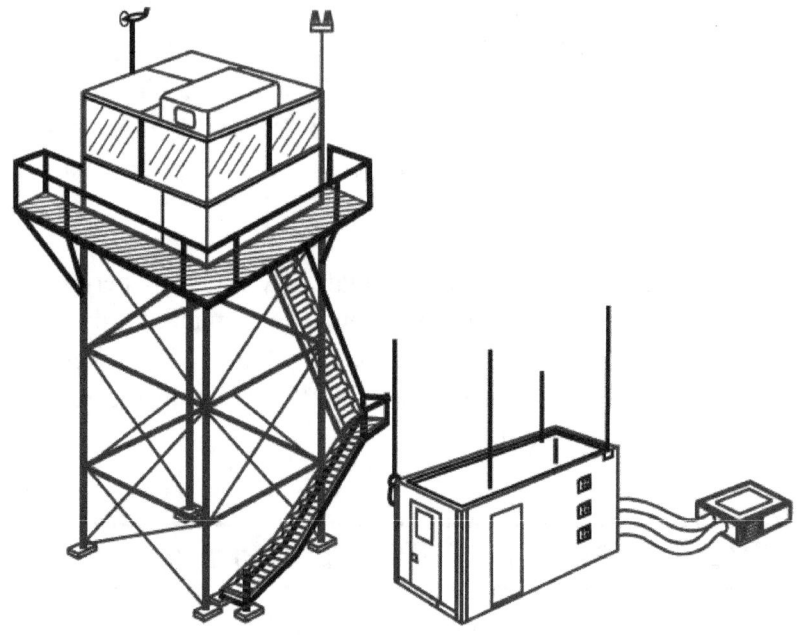

**Figure 2-4. AN/TSQ-120A/B Air Traffic
Control Central.**

AN/TRN-44A Tactical Air Navigation (TACAN) Set

The AN/TRN-44A TACAN (figure 2-5) is a transportable, dual-channel navigational aid, which provides 100 TACAN-equipped aircraft with range, bearing, and station identification information within an effective radius coverage of 200 miles. It is used for an en route navigation guidance and an instrument approach aid. The AN/TRN-44A TACAN can be erected to heights of 6, 12, 18, 24, and 30 feet.

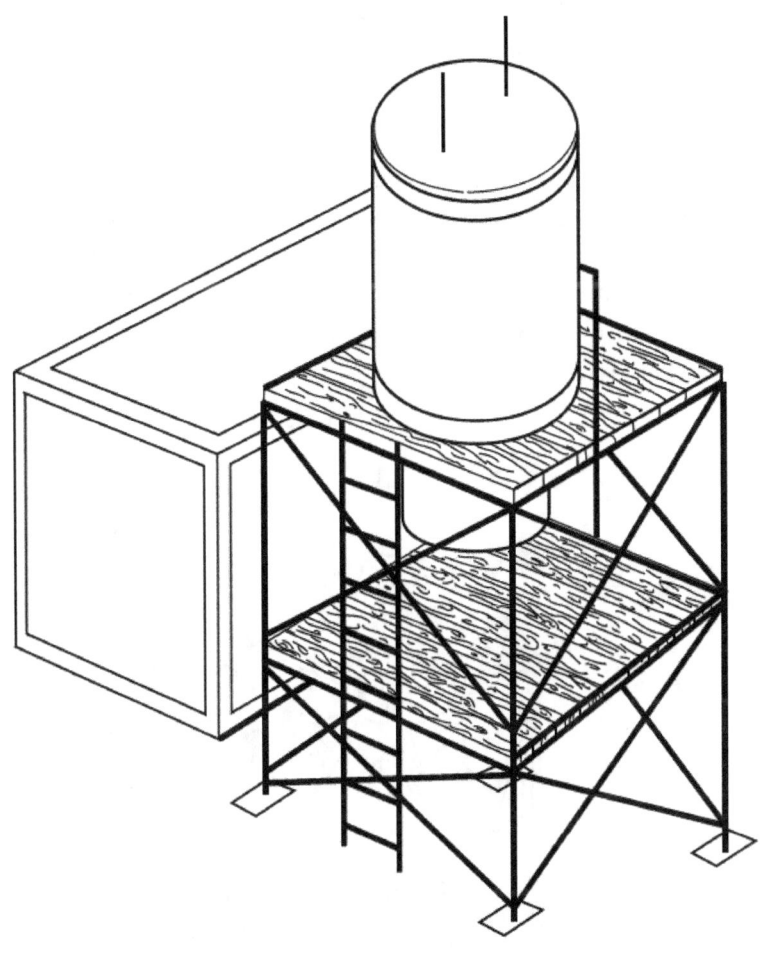

Figure 2-5. AN/TRN-44 TACAN.

AN/TPN-30A Marine Remote Area Approach and Landing System (MRAALS) with TACAN Modification

The AN/TPN-30A MRAALS (figure 2-6) is a two-person, portable, all-weather instrument landing system. It provides a 40-degree azimuth and 20-degree elevation guidance out to 10 nmi on final approach to aircraft equipped with an ARA-63 airborne radar system. It also provides 360-degree TACAN information out to 40 nmi.

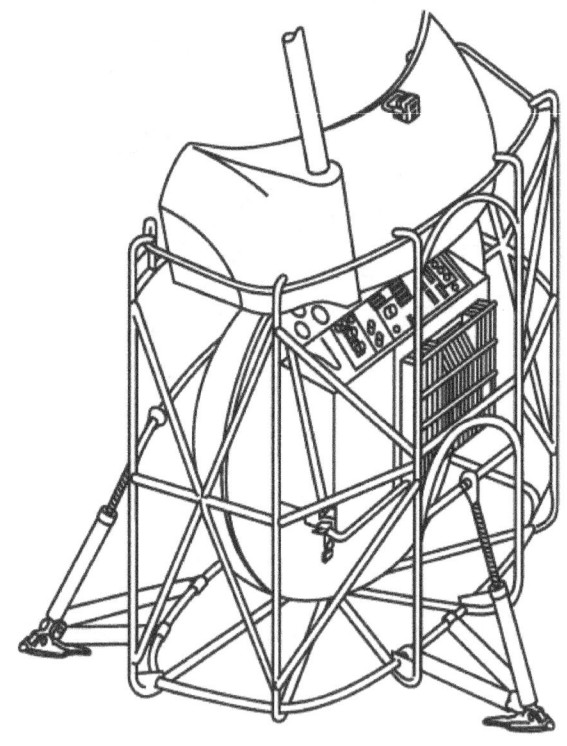

Figure 2-6. AN/TPN-30A MRAALS.

AN/TRN-46

The AN/TRN-46 is a stand-alone, man portable TACAN mounted upon a tripod. It is capable of providing TACAN information out to 40 nmi. It is lighter in weight than the TACAN modified TPN-30A, and is the preferred NAVAID for foot-mobile and air insert MMT operations.

Note: The TPN-30A and the AN/TRN-46 are not capable of being flight certified due their +/- 5 degrees accuracy in azimuth and lack of a self-monitoring capability. However, both systems can provide valuable navigation assistance in austere environments where other systems are not available. Both systems are powered by an MEP-531 generator, shore power or slaved to a tactical vehicle.

AN/TSQ-216 Remote Landing Site Tower

The RLST (figure 2-7, page 2-10) provides for the rapid emplacement, establishment, and withdrawal of extended range communications and other capabilities required for VFR ATC services at remote landing sites. The RLST consists of an extendable roof shelter containing the equipment required for ATC operations at remote sites. The system includes a highly mobile trailer to carry antennas, generators, and communications equipment. The RLST is capable of operating in a high mobility multipurpose wheeled vehicle (HMMWV) mounted configuration or in a stand alone configuration. The RLST has one HF, two VHF, and three UHF radios and the capability to introduce up to six telephone lines into its communications system. This system is HAVEQUICK and SINCGARS capable.

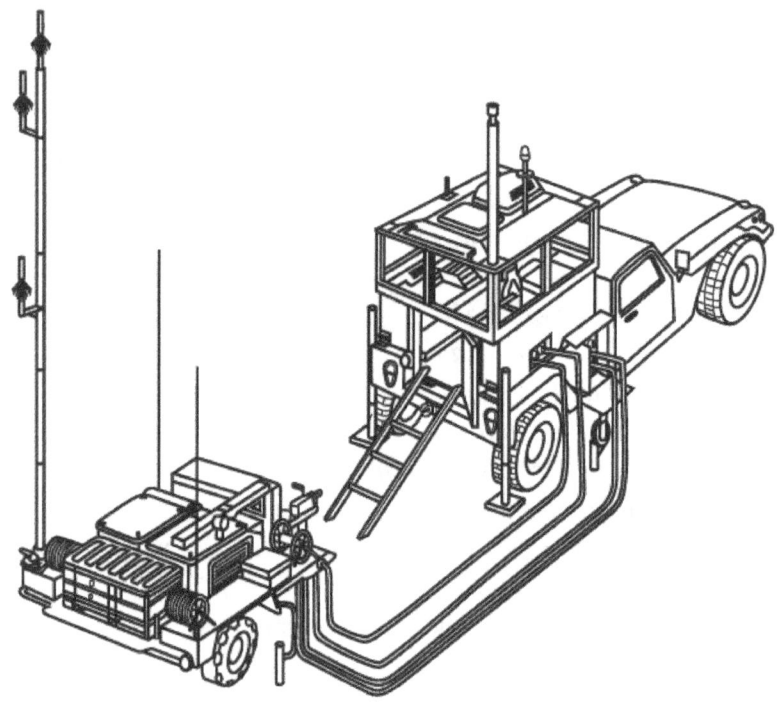

Figure 2-7. Remote Landing Site Tower.

AN/TSM-170 Maintenance Repair Group

The AN/TSM-170 consists of four shelters that contain work-benches, test equipment, cabinets, tools and other equipment nec-essary for maintenance of ATC equipment.

MEP-006A Generator/Mobile Electric Power

The MATCD provides 60-hertz (Hz) mobile electric power to support detachment operations.

Environmental Control Unit

The HD-1099 environmental control unit is used with MATCD electronic equipment shelters for cooling and heating.

LIMITATIONS

Electronic Signature

The MATCD has a large electronic signature generated by its air surveillance radars and voice data communications equipment. Effective planning and employment of EMCON measures are paramount to maximizing the MATCD's survivability.

Low Altitude Air Surveillance

Because the MATCD employs ground surveillance radar systems, its radar coverage is susceptible to line of sight (LOS) limitations. Use of high ground for radar emplacement, airborne sensors, dispersions of sensors, and incorporation of other unit's air picture can be used to minimize terrain masking effects on the MATCD.

Dispersion

The MATCD must contend with physical limitations of the equipment when considering options for dispersal. Dispersion between each radar and the CCS is restricted to the 500 foot length of the connecting cable.

Internal and External Airfield Communications

Although the MATCD has robust organic communications assets, it still requires communications support to interface with the MACCS and airfield agencies. Marine wing support squadron provides all communications internal to airfield operations at a forward operating base. Marine wing communications squadron normally provides all communications assets required to integrate within the MACCS to include multichannel communications. Depending upon the operation, support from one or both of these squadrons may be necessary for MATCD operations.

EQUIPMENT UPGRADES AND REPLACEMENTS

Among the planned improvements to Marine ATC equipment are three principal initiatives: AN/TPY-1 Tactical Terminal Control System (Overall System), commonly referred to as the air surveillance and precision approach radar control system (ASPARCS); common aviation command and control system (CAC2S); and joint precision approach landing system (JPALS).

AN/TPY-1 Tactical Terminal Control System (Overall System)

The tactical terminal control system is designed to replace the MATCALS system to provide a rapidly deployable surveillance and precision approach radar system. The tactical terminal control system will consist of three HMMWVs with trailers and required logistics support vehicles. Capable of rapidly deploying via C-130 or USMC KC-130 transport aircraft, the AN/TPY-1 will provide the Marine Corps with the capability to provide surveillance coverage and ATC services to 60 nmi and 60,000 feet above ground level in instrument meteorological conditions with minimal footprint. This will dramatically decrease the need for heavy lift assets to deploy MATCDs into a theater. The subsytems that compose the AN/TPY-1 Tactical Terminal Control System are shown in figure 2-8, page 2-14.

Common Aviation Command and Control System

Upon the end of its service life, the AN/TSQ-131 CCS will be replaced with CAC2S and the CAC2S communications suite. CAC2S will work with the tactical terminal control system to provide a common equipment suite, thus enhancing interoperability and reducing logistical requirements. CAC2S's standardized hardware suite will be equipped with a MACCS common compliment of services, workstations, processors, etc. CAC2S's software will consist of standardized common components with agency specific (TACC, TAOC, DASC, ATC, etc.) applications. Each system will be modular in design and configured to meet each agency's mission requirements.

Joint Precision Approach Landing System

JPALS will provide precision approach capability at an airstrip, airbase or expeditionary field with limited infrastructure. JPALS will be a rapidly deployable, global positioning system-based precision approach system, designed to land aircraft during instrument meteorological conditions.

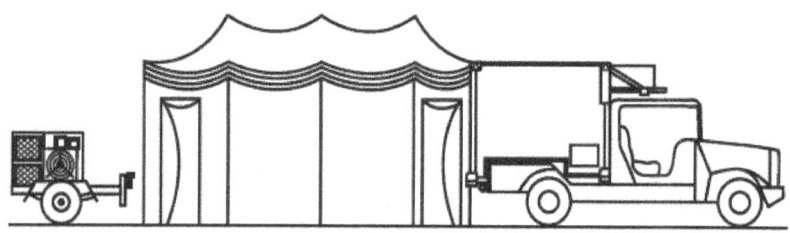

AN/TSQ-230 Tactical Terminal Control Subsystem (OS/CS)

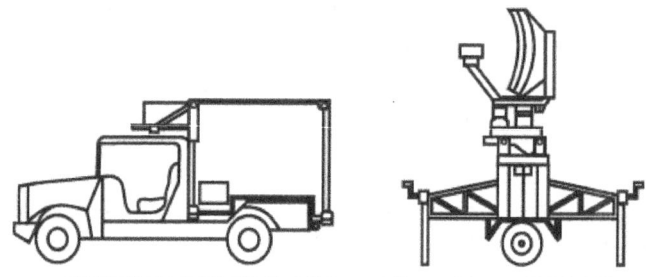

AN/TPS-79 RADAR Set (Airport Surveillance RADAR)

AN/TPN-32 Ground Control Approach Subsystem
(Precision Approach RADAR)

Figure 2-8. AN/TPY-1 Tactical Terminal Control System (Overall System).

CHAPTER 3
PLANNING

Specific information on the MAGTF planning process and the documents useful in conducting MAGTF and aviation combat element (ACE) planning are contained in FMFM 3-1, *Command and Staff Action*; MCWP 5-1, *Marine Corps Planning Process*, MCWP 5-11.1, *MAGTF Aviation Planning;* MCRP 5-11.1A, *MAGTF Aviation Planning Documents;* and Marine Corps Order (MCO) 3501.9B, *Marine Corps Combat Readiness Evaluation System; Volume VIII; The Marine Air Command and Control System (MACCS),* outlines MATCD specific planning requirements. Though the planning phases outlined in this chapter may occur in sequence, most of these steps are conducted concurrently.

INITIAL PLANNING

Considerations for the initial planning phase include—

- Conducting a mission analysis, including specified and implied tasks, based on the MAGTF and ACE commanders' intent and concept of operations.

- Identifying assumptions necessary for continuation of the planning process. These assumptions should supplement assumptions already addressed by higher headquarters and be in concert with the planning guidance received by higher headquarters.

- Analyzing the friendly force composition from the joint/multinational level down to the MACCS and addressing integration/interface requirements with the MAGTF and/or joint force planners (specifically the airspace control authority [ACA], the area air defense commander [AADC], and adjacent air control agencies).

• Conducting initial coordination/liaison with the ICAO, HN ATC facilities, and the FAA for airspace and liaison requirements.

• Analyzing the threat's air and ground order of battle (OOB) and electronic warfare (EW), reconnaissance, and unconventional warfare capabilities.

• Analyzing the amphibious objective area (AOA)/area of operations (AO), with particular emphasis on the ACA's guidance to begin initial planning for terminal control airspace, Class D airspace, and minimum-risk routes (MRRs). Class D airspace is that airspace from the surface to 2,500 feet above the airport elevation surrounding those airports/airfields that have an operational control tower.

• Identifying communications requirements for subordinate, adjacent, and higher level circuits with the ACE/MAGTF communications planners. Initial communications planning should focus on the critical information flow and the desired connectivity necessary to achieve this flow.

• Providing ATC specialist input to aviation estimates of supportability for all assigned operations. Input should summarize significant aviation aspects of the situation that might influence any course of action (COA) proposals. The input is also used to evaluate and determine how aviation units can best be employed to support contemplated MAGTF COAs. The aviation estimate is prepared by the ACE commander, his staff, and subordinate elements. The end product of the aviation estimates of supportability includes recommending a

COA to the MAGTF commander. At a minimum, aviation estimates of supportability includes—

- Which contemplated COA(s) can best be supported by the ACE.

- Salient disadvantages of less desirable COAs.

- Significant aviation limitations (including C2) and problems of an operational or logistical nature.

INTELLIGENCE PLANNING

MATCD personnel will coordinate intelligence planning with the squadron intelligence staff (S-2) or higher headquarters. Intelligence planning considerations include—

- Obtaining preliminary and detailed aviation intelligence estimates.

- Identifying intelligence requirements (IRs) and submitting them to the squadron S-2 in the form of simple and concise requests. IRs should state the preferred product format.

- Determining the MATCD staff's requirements for maps, charts, photographs, and other graphic aids.

- Obtaining a complete enemy OOB including information on the threat's missiles, aviation assets, EW, naval, and ground force capabilities.

- Preparing a detailed rear area assessment for the MATCD and any deployed sites within its assigned sector.

- Determining the enemy's access to and the overhead times for satellite systems and the enemy's processing time for the imagery.

COMMUNICATIONS PLANNING

Communications planning involves a coordinated effort between MATCD/MACS representatives and communications planners within the MACCS and ACE/MAGTF staffs. Communications planning considerations include—

- Establishing required communications connectivity between adjacent MACCS agencies, and agencies external and internal to the supported airfield (including civil ATC agencies).

- Determining required communications nets, and a prioritization and restoration plan for their use. Appendix B provides a list of communications nets used by the MATCD.

- Determining data link connectivity requirements for TADIL B and TADIL C.

- Developing a security control of air traffic and navigation aids (SCATANA) plan. The SCATANA plan includes procedures for silent aircraft taxi, launch, and recovery procedures for day and night operations; NAVAIDS which will be secured; and the securing authority for the NAVAIDS.

- Identifying communications security material. Planners should address required encryption hardware and software, authentication tables, brevity codes, and challenge/password changeover times.

- Ensuring the MATCD is included on distribution lists for the automated communications electronics operating instruction and airspace control order/air tasking order (ACO/ATO).

- Addressing ATC unique frequency requirements with ACE/ MAGTF communications planners. The necessity for like communications media between the MATCD and civil aviation authorities requires MATCD planning for using frequencies within the VHF(AM) frequency spectrum (116 to 134 MHz with 50-kilohertz [kHz] spacings). This frequency band is used for the control of civil aircraft; 50-kHz spacing may also be necessary for the UHF band for communicating with allied nations' aircraft.

ELECTRONIC WARFARE PLANNING

When the enemy has a known EW and electronics intelligence capability, planning considerations include—

- Requesting an assessment of the enemy's electronic OOB (communications and radar jamming capabilities, antiradiation missile capabilities, and delivery profiles).

- Submitting recommendations for EMCON and radiation control (RADCON) standards within the MATCD's assigned sector. EMCON and RADCON plans should incorporate all ground-based sensors operating within the sector and consider the antiradiation missile threat to maintain effective sector surveillance. EMCON and RADCON planning considerations should address—

  - Minimum communications procedures.

  - Use of brevity codes and authentication devices.

  - Use and security of communications security (COMSEC) materials.

  - Delegation of EMCON authority.

- Signals security.

- Beadwindow calls.

- Gingerbread procedures.

- Employment of directional antennas.

- Circuit discipline.

- Appropriate radio wattage.

- Radar blinking and blanking.

- Use of frequency diversity and frequency agile radios.

- Physical dispersion and appropriate siting of communications emitters (including radars, radios, and NAVAIDS).

- Available demand features on NAVAIDS and their use.

- Considering the EW threat when determining the locations of MATCD radars.

- Providing input to the MAGTF C2 warfare plan.

- Ensuring that planners, operators, and users of electronic equipment thoroughly understand the EW threat and the EMCON/EP techniques used to counter that threat.

SITE SELECTION PLANNING

The site selection planning process begins once the MATCD's sector is assigned. Planners must ensure adequate space for site establishment, access to the site, and radar coverage of the sector are maximized. The site selection planning process includes—

- Conducting surveys using maps, aerial photos, charts, and other graphic aids to identify candidate sites.

- Producing/obtaining radar coverage diagrams from the tactical aviation mission planning system, Joint Electronics Office, portable flight planning system (PFPS), other automated sources or manual computations.

- Determining optimum siting locations for communications connectivity with higher/adjacent and subordinate agencies using applicable computer programs, LOS diagrams, and HF propagation predictions.

- Submitting a list of candidate sites to the ACE commander based on map surveys and other studies. MATCD siting considerations should encompass all task-organized equipment and personnel in movement and physical requirements. Physical site characteristics considerations include—

  - Radar coverage of the assigned airspace.

  - Ground that has no more than 10 degrees of slope.

  - Spatial requirements; e.g., antennas or radio frequency hazards.

  - Logistics supportability.

  - Camouflage and concealment.

  - Trafficability and access.

  - Emergency destruction and/or movement.

  - Drainage.

  - Defensibility.

- In addition to the physical geography of the site, planners should consider the candidate site's proximity to related activities occurring in or around the FOB. These functional site considerations should address the locations of—

  - Fuel points and fuel storage areas.

  - Ordnance storage areas.

- Arming/dearming areas.

- Air lift control element locations.

- Pre-existing NAVAIDS.

- Arresting gear.

- Casualty evacuation areas.

- Search and rescue aircraft.

- Crash, fire, and rescue units/hot spots.

- Field weather observation services.

- Field of view.

- Obstructions.

- Requesting radar frequency authorization from the appropriate authorities.

- Establishing a phased plan of equipment arrival at the site to facilitate rapid commencement of operational capabilities and communications.

- Selecting an advanced party to conduct physical reconnaissance, locate positions for equipment, and plan specific equipment sites.

- Preparing diagrams or models that depict equipment locations and are the basis for setup crew briefings.

- Ensuring site plans consider maximum dispersal and remoting of equipment to reduce electromagnetic and infrared signatures.

- Designating alternate site locations.

AIRSPACE MANAGEMENT PLANNING

Airspace management planning involves segmenting assigned airspace by volume and/or time for the safe and expeditious flow of air traffic. Airspace management planning also involves establishing various air defense control measures designed to protect friendly installations from enemy air attack. Planning considerations include—

- Analyzing the AOA/AO to determine dimensions, suitable airfields within, possible conflicts with civil aviation, unmanned aerial vehicles (UAVs), and preferred routings for friendly aircraft.

- Determining the size and shape of terminal control airspace. Usable NAVAIDS, civil air traffic patterns, UAVs, and conflicts with other users of this airspace will affect the airspace's configuration.

- Determining the size and shape of Class D airspace. Military (manned and unmanned aircraft) and applicable civil traffic patterns should be considered.

- Ascertaining the size and shape of the BDZ. BDZ dimensions are normally determined by the effective engagement envelope of the supporting air defense systems; e.g., Stinger and anticipated air traffic patterns. Entry and exit procedures, including safe lanes and IFF mode and code requirements, must be established during BDZ construction.

- Coordinating with local ground-based air defense unit(s) for BDZ early warning cueing.

- Preparing TERPs for designated airfields and submitting the approach plates to the Naval Flight Information Group for approval and publication.

- Participating with other MACCS agencies in the planning and development of MRRs. Planning should include consideration of UAV and civil aircraft routing.

- Coordinating with ICAO, HN ATC, and/or FAA authorities for the effective use of existing airspace.

- Coordinating with higher headquarters to publish ATC procedures in the ACO/airspace control plan (ACP) and pilot controller handbook.

- Developing procedures for handling transient aircraft within the MAGTF/joint AO.

EXTERNAL SUPPORT PLANNING

MATCD-unique external support planning considerations include—

- Identifying and coordinating sufficient transportation and materials handling equipment necessary to rapidly emplace the MATCD.

- Coordinating aviation supply/logistics support for Naval Air Systems Command-supported equipment through the MALS.

- Multichannel communications support for data link operations.

- Ground security requirements.

JOINT/MULTINATIONAL OPERATIONS PLANNING

The MAGTF must ensure its operations are integrated and coordinated with joint/multinational forces. MAGTF air C2 representatives should be included as part of the joint operations planning; e.g., development of the joint air operations plan, ACP or the air defense plan. The ACE commander, his staff, and/or MACCS agencies normally provide these subject matter experts. They also identify MAGTF capabilities and requirements relative to airspace control and air defense operations. Joint/multinational operations plans must specifically—

- Integrate with and complement the joint/multinational force's mission.

- Ensure the interoperability of equipment and personnel.

- Ensure the common use and understanding of terminology.

- Allow responsiveness and the massing of firepower whenever and wherever needed.

- Identify the proper liaison and staff/agency representation between joint force components. Representatives from each component must enable and improve the information flow and provide expertise.

- Outline procedures for airspace control and air defense degradation.

- Facilitate transition from peacetime conditions to hostilities.

- Delineate logistical support.

Air operations, airspace, and air defense planning will be integrated with the joint force's planning cycle. Input from all components must be consolidated and integrated into the joint air operations plan, the ACP, and the air defense plan. The ACP and air defense plan are part of the joint air operations plan and must be included in the joint force operations plan. The ACO is published and disseminated based on guidelines established in the ACP. As an integral part of the joint ATO, integrated tasking order or air tasking message (North Atlantic Treaty Organization [NATO]), the ACO may be distributed as a part of these documents or may be issued separately.

OPERATIONS BRIEF

The MATCD operations brief is developed based on the planning conducted at the MACC; e.g., Marine air control group (MACG) planning staff level. It ensures that the detachment has sufficient information to prepare for operations at its FOB. The brief may serve as an additional source of information along with operations orders, the ACP, the ACO, and applicable standing operating procedures (SOPs) for supervisors to prepare crew briefings before assuming their watch. Appendix C is an operations brief format.

CHAPTER 4
OPERATIONS

The MAGTF commander uses Marine aviation to assist efforts to support the commander, amphibious task force; naval expeditionary force commander; joint task force commander; or joint force commander. In its most common employment, the MATCD will operate to support expeditionary operations ashore.

EMPLOYMENT

MATCD training standards are detailed in appendix D. The MATCD task-organizes to fulfill its mission. The services required at an FOB will dictate the number of personnel and types of equipment necessary to support the mission. Common MATCD employment options follow.

Full Service ATC Detachment

The full service ATC detachment is designed to support continuous all-weather ATC services at a main air base. Services provided by the full service ATC detachment typically include tower control, TACAN, radar approach and departure control, and precision/non-precision and instrument approaches. Table 4-1 on page 4-2 is a notional equipment listing for a full service ATC detachment.

Table 4-1. Full Service ATC Detachment Notional Equipment Listing.

System	Nomenclature	Quantity
AN/TSQ-120B	ATC Tower	1
AN/TRN-44	TACAN	1
AN/TPN-22	Precision Approach Radar	1
AN/TPS-73	Airport Surveillance Radar	1
AN/TSQ-131	Communication Control Subsystem	2
AN/TPN-30A	MRAALS (Microwave Landing System)	2
AN/TRN-46	TACAN (man portable)	3
OA-9141/TSM-170	Auxiliary Equipment Maintenance Facility	1
OA-9142/TSM-170	Communications Equipment Maintenance Facility	1
OA-9143/TSM-170	Radar Equipment Maintenance Facility	1
OA-9144/TSM-170	Microcomputer Repair Facility	1
HD-1099	Environmental Control Unit	18
MEP006A	Generator Set	11
MEP531	Generator Set	5

Tower and TACAN Detachment

The tower and TACAN detachment capabilities focus on providing all-weather ATC services at a designated site. Services provided by the tower and TACAN detachment include control tower and TACAN instrument approaches and departures. Table 4-2 is a notional equipment listing for a tower and TACAN detachment.

Table 4-2. Tower and TACAN Detachment Notional Equipment Listing.

System	Nomenclature	Quantity
AN/TSQ-120 A/B	ATC Tower	1
AN/TRN-44	TACAN	1
OA-9144/TSM-170	Communications Equipment Maintenance Facility	1
HD-1099	Environmental Control Unit	5

MMT

The MMT is used for short duration operations, typically 72 hours or less, as the lead element of a follow-on detachment. An MMT can provide positive and procedural ATC services up to 40 nmi from a TLZ using portable NAVAIDS. The MMT's small logistics footprint requires fewer transportation assets than the larger MATCD options and is conducive to rapid site establishment and retrograde. Table 4-3 on page 4-4 is a notional equipment configuration for the MMT.

Table 4-3. MMT
Notional Equipment Listing.

System	Nomenclature	Quantity
AN/TPN-30/AN/ TRN-46	MRAALS (Microwave Landing System) or Distance and Measuring Equipment	1
MEP531	Generator Set	1
AN/PRC-117F	UHF/VHF Radio	3
AN/PRC-150	HF Radio	1
TA-312	Field Phone	2
CYZ-10/KYK-13	Fill Device	1
KY-57	Transmission Security (TSEC) Device	2
KY-99	TSEC Device	1
ACR/L-32	Light Set	1
----	Hand-Held Anemometer	1
----	Portable Aldis Lamp	1
----	Pyrotechnic Pistol	1
----	70 x 50 Binoculars	1
TSQ-216	RLST*	1
MM1038	HMMWV**	1 or 2

* The RLST is employed by one of the two organic detachment MMTs.
**HMMWVs and RLSTs are not normally used on heliborne inserts.

CONCEPT OF EMPLOYMENT

The MATCD task-organizes its personnel and assets to support its MAGTF/joint assigned mission. While a particular MATCD configuration may normally be associated with a Marine expeditionary force (MEF) or Marine expeditionary unit (special operations capable) (MEU[SOC]), specific requirements for a given tactical situation will dictate the actual configuration suitable for the mission.

MARINE EXPEDITIONARY FORCE

Coordination of MAGTF air operations during MEF operations requires a considerable amount of ATC support and will typically be based on the number of airbases and FOBs from which MAGTF aircraft are operating. Normally, three full MATCDs will deploy to provide continuous, all-weather ATC services at up to three main airbases. The three detachments can also field six MMTs to provide limited ATC services at air facilities or air sites. Marine expeditionary brigade elements are typically supported by two MATCDs. The two detachments can provide continuous, fully capable ATC services for two main airbases and four MMTs for ATC support at four air facilities or air sites.

MEU(SOC)

Limited ATC services are typically provided to a MEU(SOC) by one MMT. The MMT is capable of controlling TLZs for fixed-wing aircraft and HLZs for rotary-wing aircraft under visual meteorological conditions and instrument meteorological conditions. The MMT has the organic capability to operate for up to 72 hours without resupply or augmentation. It can support a variety of ATC missions as an independent unit or as part of a larger force in joint/multinational operations. Specifics regarding MMT employment are discussed in the Marine aviation weapons and tactics squadron (MAWTS)-1 MMT SOPs and unit SOPs.

The MMT is specifically designed to be inserted in remote locations to support MAGTF air operations. Common methods of MMT insertion are tactical vehicle and air insert. To move personnel and equipment to the air point, each MMT is assigned per T/E with a HMMWV. Normally, all MMT personnel and equipment fit within the HMMWV.

Air insert operations deliver the MMT to their assigned air point by fixed-wing/rotary-wing aircraft. The MMT is among the first aviation capabilities introduced into the objective area. Early establishment of ATC services at the air point ensures that all succeeding aviation efforts have ATC and navigational guidance available, thus enhancing the safe and expeditious flow of air traffic into and out of the air point and surrounding airspace.

MATCD/MACCS INTERAGENCY RELATIONS

MATCD and TACC

The MATCD is subordinate to the TACC and provides decentralized control functions for friendly air traffic operating in and around designated forward operating bases. Through liaisons to HN ATC facilities and operational detachments established at

FOBs, MATCD personnel keep the TACC informed on the status of friendly and civilian air traffic, changes to airspace control measures that impact air operations, and the operational status of various airbases/airfields. The TACC provides the MATCD with guidance on the conduct of MAGTF air operations and updates to the ATO and ACO.

MATCD and TAOC

The MATCD and TAOC coordinate aircraft departure and return to force information to assist in the aircraft identification and recovery process. The TAOC advises the MATCD on the current air defense warning conditions and threat information for the MATCD activation and control of the BDZ. The MATCD disseminates air defense control measures received from the TAOC to applicable MAGTF elements and aircraft under MATCD control.

MATCD and DASC

The MATCD and DASC coordinate aircraft departure and return to force information to assist in the aircraft identification and recovery process.

MATCD and LAAD/Short Range Air Defense

The MATCD and short range air defense (SHORAD) units coordinate the BDZ that surrounds an FOB. Surveillance radar is used to cue air defense assets and threat aircraft are engaged according to the rules of engagement to defend the FOB. Although the MATCD normally coordinates with the Marine LAAD battalion, US Army, HN, and coalition SHORAD weapons may also be used in a BDZ.

MATCD and the Airboss

MATCD works closely with the airboss at a FOB to coordinate air operations. Operational information concerning aircraft status, the launching of alert aircraft, and flight plans are coordinated to ensure efficient flight operations.

OPERATIONAL REQUIREMENTS

Each MATCD has the capability of supporting one main airbase and two remote air sites or points. The detachment has a full range of ATC capabilities to include air surveillance radar, IFF, ACLS radar, communications, NAVAIDs, and a control tower. This equipment provides a MATCD with positive airspace control capabilities that encompass airspace extending out to 60 nmi from a main air base using radar control procedures and out to the limits of MATCD designated airspace using nonradar procedures (procedural control). To maximize the capabilities of the MATCD, the following general operational requirements should be considered.

Emplacement

The safe conduct of ATC services is predicated on the controllers' ability to detect aircraft and communicate with the aircrew. The location of ATC equipment plays a significant role in facilitating these services.

Terminal Instrument Procedures

Following selection of an airfield, determination of the level of ATC services, and selection of MATCD equipment locations, airfield instrument approaches are developed to ensure obstruction clearance is adequate. Once instrument approach procedures are developed, they are sent to the Naval Flight Information Group for approval. A notice to airmen is disseminated until published in the flight information publication. Each detachment maintains at least one resident TERP specialist.

> *Note: An airfield site survey team to include a TERP specialist(s) should be sent ahead of the advanced party or at a minimum as part of the advanced party prior to the MATCD deployment. This is to ensure the timely and accurate gathering of information to meet ATC specific requirements in the development of ATC procedures.*

Flight Inspection

A flight check of ATC instrument approaches is required by the FAA. The check is normally conducted by an FAA flight check aircraft. When an FAA flight check aircraft is not available, the ACE commander may authorize a military aircraft to conduct the flight check in accordance with FAA publication AO P8200.1, *Flight Inspection Manual*. This alternative will allow MAGTF aircraft to use the instrument approaches until an FAA flight check is successfully completed.

MATCD IN AMPHIBIOUS/EXPEDITIONARY OPERATIONS

MATCD elements, notably the MMT and liaisons, are typically among the first MACCS air control capabilities introduced ashore. MMTs, used in a stand-alone role or as a precursor for a buildup for a larger MATCD, are initially established to coincide with initiation of FOB air operations. As airfields are secured, additional ATC capabilities may be phased into the AOA/AO to provide additional, continuous ATC services for US Marine Corps, joint, and allied Services' aircraft operating from AOA/AO airfields. When MAGTF aviation elements are forward based at an allied nation's airfield located near the AOA/AO, MATCD personnel may be assigned as liaisons to the HN's ATC adminis-tration. With the introduction of ATC radars into the MAGTF's AO, the MATCD will coordinate the requisite voice and data links necessary to contribute to the force's IADS through the Marine or Navy sector antiair warfare coordinator or the antiair warfare commander.

JOINT/MULTINATIONAL OPERATIONS

The MATCD's role in joint/multinational operations differs little from amphibious/expeditionary operations. The MATCD will support MAGTF air operations and integrate with the joint/multi-national force. Marine ATC coordination with the ACA for the promulgation of airspace control measures and airfield rules is a high priority for MACCS operations. Of equal significance is the role MATCD controllers play as liaisons to allied ATC facilities to facilitate the coordination of MAGTF airspace. MATCD per-sonnel may be functioning from airfields used by joint and allied

Service aircraft. Versatility, familiarity, and experience in joint/ multinational ATC and airfield procedures is paramount to enhancing aircrew safety and success.

MILITARY OPERATIONS OTHER THAN WAR

The MATCD is capable of deploying and operating independent of the MAGTF, joint force, or joint task force to provide ATC support for various types of operations other than war. Examples of this type of ATC support are providing ATC and C3 services to assist domestic and foreign humanitarian efforts, NEOs, assisting other joint/allied Services, and supporting intergovernmental ATC requirements. For limited duration operations, MMT can provide robust air traffic capability with a dramatically smaller footprint at airfields to support military operations other than war.

VOICE COMMUNICATIONS

The MATCD is a communications-intensive agency. A typical voice communications configuration for a MATCD includes air-to-ground communications with aircraft, and ground-to-ground communications with MACCS, joint, and multinational/host nation air control agencies. Appendix B lists the communications nets commonly used by the MATCD. Communications planners should consider that while secure voice communications may be used in support of tactical operations, communications with civil aircraft must be conducted on nonsecure circuits.

DATA LINK COMMUNICATIONS

Expediency in reporting air tracks and updating track positions is crucial to effective air defense operations. The MATCD contributes to the MAGTF's overall air picture development through air track exchange over digital data links.

MATCALS is capable of exchanging track data information over one TADIL B data link with another TADIL B-capable air C2 agency, such as the Marine TACC or TAOC. If the second TADIL B reporting unit is conducting TADIL operations with other air C2 agencies, air tracks initiated by the MATCD can be forwarded to other participating data link agencies, and the MATCD can receive tracks forwarded from the other air C2 agencies.

This exchange of track information greatly enhances situational awareness for all participating agencies and significantly assists in the identification of friendly aircraft, thus reducing chances of fratricide. Voice reporting (cross tell/voice tell) of air tracks may be used to supplement the data link picture or when the data link is inoperative.

EQUIPMENT SELECTION AND EMPLACEMENT CONSIDERATIONS

Upon receipt of a warning order or after initial tasking, MATCD planners begin determining the equipment needed to support operations.

Generally, equipment requirements are based on the detachment's mission, location(s), available lift and logistics support, anticipated duration, and space available at the site. The MATCD commander and maintenance officer will typically weigh these factors against historical data to determine the equipment suites necessary to support operations, necessary maintenance facilities, mobile electric power support, and parts pack-up. The initial equipment plan is briefed to the MACS commanding officer for initial approval. Specific concerns for selecting potential sites that follow apply to all MATCD operations, whether the MATCD is operating in a garrison or tactical situation.

SURVEYS

The two types of surveys necessary for determining the equipment needed to support operations are the map survey and the physical survey.

Map Survey

The map survey is normally conducted concurrently with initial equipment planning. Map surveys of potential airfields/air sites are used to gain an initial impression of the surrounding terrain, runways, taxiways, and parking aprons, and to determine how these factors influence MATCD equipment siting and air traffic flow. The goal of the map survey is to ascertain the practicality of providing unobstructed "views" for the tower and radars and to identify potential locations for the detachment's equipment and maximizing ATC procedures. Key considerations to be addressed during the map survey include identification of the limitations on equipment separation based on cable length, safety zones around radiation hazards, and potential of electromagnetic interference from other radio-electronic sources. Often imagery may be more current and accurate than map data and may be used for survey of nondepicted manmade objects. It is often preferred for initial site.

Physical Survey

When practical, a physical site survey should be conducted to confirm or refute site locations identified during the map survey. The physical survey affords MATCD personnel the opportunity to update site information that was not available from a map, adjust equipment locations; and determine the types of support, such as commercial power and telephone access, available at the airfield/air site. Physical site surveys conducted by qualified MATCD personnel are recommended prior to deployment of the detachment's equipment.

EQUIPMENT EMPLACEMENT

When conducting the map and physical surveys and during the actual equipment emplacement, MATCD Marines should consider unique properties associated with the various equipment.

AN/TSQ-120 (ATC Control Tower)

When erecting the control tower, priority should be given to the controller's field of vision. A clear view of runways, movement areas, and approach surfaces is paramount. Tower personnel should have unobstructed views of taxiways, ramp areas, and arming/dearming sites to enhance safe movement in and around the airfield. The tower requires a 10- by 15-foot level area with firm soil for erection. Tower height should be kept as low as practical to reduce its vulnerability as a target.

AN/TRN-44A (TACAN)

The TACAN is an LOS transmitter. Antenna height is determined by local terrain and obstacles. Like the control tower, it should be raised no higher than necessary. To achieve the best approach possible (a straight-in approach to minimums of 1 mile and 500 feet), the TACAN must be located within 1 mile of the airport reference point. The site should be a clear, flat area free of obstructions; e.g., buildings or trees, for 1/4 mile if possible. Hard surfaces; e.g., runways or taxiways, especially if constructed of metal matting, should be avoided due to reflections that distort the TACAN's pattern.

RADARS

Emplacement of the radars is generally more difficult than the other equipment suites due to their susceptibility to terrain effects, necessary logistics support, power/generator requirements, and limitations to interface with other equipment suites.

An operational analysis of the airfield, number of approaches to different runways, number of touchdown points, and desired landing minimums should be made before selecting radar sites. The primary instrument runway is selected after taking into account factors such as weather, terrain, and obstacles. Normally, this runway will have the least restrictive (lowest) landing minimums. Secondary instrument runways and their attendant touchdown points are identified and covered if possible.

Two key factors for radar site consideration are the landing operations to be supported and physical and electromagnetic effects on a radar's tracking. The airport surveillance radar must be placed such that radar blind spots are eliminated. The precision approach radar must be sited to maximize coverage and preclude drop-tracks due to clutter. The approach corridor for the primary instrument runway should be free of obstructions. The TPN-22 precision approach radar's siting is the most critical as it provides terminal guidance for aircraft landing in adverse weather and/or poor visibility situations.

APPENDIX A
FORWARD OPERATING BASES

MAGTF aviation operates from sea- or shore-based airfields close to or within its AOs. When operating ashore, MAGTF aviation uses FOBs to support tactical operations without establishing full support facilities. FOBs increase responsiveness through basing flexibility and aircraft dispersal and by decreasing distances to support areas.

The distinguishing characteristic among the various MAGTF airfields is the services that are available at a given type of airbase. The maintenance functions and sustainability aspects, not the method of construction, give each type of FOB its specific definition. Classifications for various FOBs follow.

MAIN AIRBASE

A main air base is a secure airfield that is capable of handling all types of aircraft, up to and including theater lift assets. A main airbase's support agencies and facilities are determined by task organization requirements but should include intermediate maintenance activity support and engineering functions necessary to support current and anticipated needs. In the classic amphibious operation, this base would be located near the coastline and integrated with the MAGTF logistics pipeline. The main airbase functions to support sustained operations ashore.

AIR FACILITY

An air facility is a secure airfield capable of supporting a detachment or squadron and its associated organizational maintenance activity. An air facility should be capable of sustained operations at a combat sortie rate and provide the support required to initially stage and later replenish forward sites.

Organizational maintenance activity support should include basic troubleshooting and repair, daily turnaround inspections, refueling, weapons loading/downloading, and arming/dearming functions. Major maintenance functions such as engine changes and phase inspections are not accomplished at an air facility unless it is more advantageous than returning the aircraft to the rear area main base or a sea base. Aviation ordnance is stored in the open, using accepted procedures. Support equipment with rough terrain capability is desirable for movement, loading, and maintenance of aircraft. An air facility might be an airfield, road segment, matted runway or in the case of vertical/short takeoff and landing aircraft and helicopters, flat ground or a grass strip.

AIR SITE

The air site is a secure location where combat aircraft are prepositioned to enhance response time. It is suitable for a fully loaded and armed aircraft to land and ground loiter awaiting a mission, either preplanned or on-call. Ideally, fuel and ordnance would be staged at this site. During normal operations, the air site requires minimal logistics support. Operations are limited to receiving and launching previously loaded aircraft and require a minimum number of support personnel. The air site has the potential to expand its capabilities to meet operational requirements. On completion of a mission from an air site, aircraft normally return to an air facility or main base for refueling, arming/dearming, and maintenance. Personnel typically required to accomplish site maintenance include a plane captain or crew chief per aircraft and one ordnance man per air site. Generally, only hand-carried support equipment and tools are required.

AIR POINT

Air points are specific predetermined geographic locations that will support a specific tactical mission. Types of air points include the FARP and the lagger point.

Forward Arming and Refueling Point

FARPs are temporary and transitory in nature and are established for a specific mission. The ultimate objective of the FARP is to minimize flight time to and from the objective area. This is accomplished by locating the FARP as close to the objective area as allowed by mission, enemy, terrain and weather, troops and support available, and time available. Normally, FARP support consists of fuel, ordnance, communications, and command element personnel. When fixed-wing assets are used, plane captains are required. Aviation maintenance conducted at a FARP should be restricted to minor repair and adjustments that can be made by the crew chief or plane captain. Equipment that normally supports the FARP should be limited to that which directly supports the mission; i.e., helicopter expeditionary refueling system, rapid ground refueling, short airfield for tactical support loaders, and other necessary ground support equipment.

Lagger Point

Lagger points are secure locations designated by aviation units for the rendezvous, marshalling or positioning of flights of aircraft between missions or when awaiting completion or activation of an assigned mission. Other than communications, no other equipment support should be required. Lagger points can be isolated or independent or they may be adjacent to a main base, air facility, air site or FARP.

APPENDIX B
COMMUNICATIONS NETS

	Purpose	Composition
Tactical Air Command/ **(VHF/HF/UHF-SATCOM)**	Provides the primary means by which the ACE commander tasks subordinate elements to meet the six functions of Marine aviation.	• Marine TACC. • Sector air defense facility. • TAOCs. • DASC. • Marine aircraft groups/ squadrons. • MATCDs. • Early warning/control (EW/C) sites. • TADIL B (CABLE/MUX)
TADIL B/(Cable/MUX)	A point-to-point, full duplex digital data link designed to exchange air track information between appropriately equipped air C2 agencies.	• Marine TACC. • TAOCs. • EW/Cs. • MATCDs. • Other Service air C2 agencies.
Track Supervision Net **(TSN) (HF/UHF/MUX)**	Provides a means for track surveillance personnel to exchange voice information to maintain a clear data link picture. This net may be used as the data link coordination net based on equipment availability.	• Marine TACC. • TAOCs. • EW/Cs • MATCDs. • Other Service data link capable air C2 agencies.
Combat Information/ **Detection Net (MUX/HF)**	Provides a means for reporting on hostile or unidentified aircraft. Multiple combat information/ detection (CI/D) nets may be required when several radar surveillance activities are employed.	• Marine TACC. • TAOCs. • EW/Cs. • MATCDs. • LAAD units. • Other surveillance agencies.

	Purpose	Composition
Air Defense Command and Control Net (SATCOM/HF/UHF)	Used by the AADC to pass tactical commands to the area air defense plan. Information passed via the air defense command and control net (ADCCN) includes, but is not limited to, weapons release conditions, alert states, missile engagement zone activation, surveillance modifications, combat air patrol station modifications, and MRR/safe corridor modifications.	• Joint interface and air defense units. • Marine TACC. • TAOCs. • EW/Cs. • MATCDs. • Other surveillance agencies.
Handover/Cross Tell (H/O/X-TELL) Net (UHF/MUX)	Provides a means to coordinate aircraft control between air control agencies. Multiple nets can be established or the functions may be combined based on traffic load.	• Composition Marine TACC. • TAOCs. • EW/Cs. • DASC. • MATCDs.
Tactical Air Traffic Control (TATC) Net (UHF/VHF)	Provides a means for the TACC/TADC, TAOC, EW/C, MATCDS, and DASC to exercise control of all tactical and itinerant aircraft in the objective area.	• Composition • Marine TACC. • TAOCs. • EW/Cs. • MATCDs. • DASC. • Direct air support center (airborne) (DASC[A]). • Fixed-wing aircraft. • Rotary-wing aircraft.

	Purpose	Composition
Guard Net (UHF/VHF)	Emergency distress net for aircraft; also used to warn aircraft of emergency conditions.	• Composition Marine TACC. • TAOCs. • EW/Cs. • DASC. • MATCDs. • Fixed-wing and rotary-wing aircraft. • Other Service air C2 agencies.
Search and Rescue Net (UHF)	Provides a means for control and coordination of search and rescue (SAR) missions. Multiple SAR nets may be required.	• All elements within the air C2 system. • Aircraft involved in SAR operations.
Aircraft Rescue and Firefighting (ARFF) Net (VHF)	Provides a means to coordinate crash recoveries on or around an airfield.	• Composition • Crash crew. • ATC facilities. • Airfield operations.
Air Traffic Control Common (MUX/HF)	Provides a means for ATC facilities to coordinate airspace management between airfields.	• Includes involved ATC facilities.

APPENDIX C
OPERATIONS BRIEF FORMAT

A. Weather

B. Intelligence/Situation Brief

    1. Enemy:

        a. Air OOB.

        b. Ground OOB.

        c. EW capabilities.

        d. Nuclear, biological, and chemical capabilities.

        e. Surface-to-surface missile threat.

        f. Terrorist threat.

    2. Friendly:

        a. FOBs.

        b. Aircraft.

        c. UAVs.

        d. Ground forces.

        e. MACCS agencies and locations.

        f. Joint/multinational air control agencies.

        g. ICAO/HN ATC agencies.

C. Commander's Intent

D. Command, Control, and Communications Plan

    1. Airspace management.

    2. AOA/AO:

        a. Approach control airspace.

        b. Class D airspace.

        c. Destruction area.

        d. BDZ.

e. Missile engagement zones.

f. Fighter engagement zones

g. Terminal control areas.

h. Routing.

i. Fixed-wing.

j. Rotary-wing.

k. UAV.

l. Civil.

m. ACP/ACO update.

n. Air defense warning conditions.

o. Lame duck procedures.

3. Communications plan:

a. Communications connectivity.

b. Required communications nets.

c. Data link.

d. EMCON/SCATANA.

e. Crypto.

E. Rules of Engagement

1. Identification authority.
2. Engagement authority.
3. Identification criteria.
4. Weapons control status.
5. Self-defense criteria.

F. Emergency Procedures

1. SAR/medical evacuation.
2. Tactical recovery of aircraft and personnel.
3. Flush plan.

G. Reports

H. Questions

APPENDIX D
TRAINING

Every Marine Corps leader has the responsibility to establish and conduct technical and tactical training to successfully accomplish the unit's mission. The complexities of amphibious, joint, multinational operations, and the importance of MATCD individual, crew, and unit level training, cannot be overstated.

INDIVIDUAL TRAINING

Air Traffic Controllers

Air traffic controller entry-level training is conducted at Naval Air Station (NAS), Pensacola. Air traffic controller training requirements, individual and crew-specific, are standardized by NAVAIR 00-80T-114, *Air Traffic Control Facilities Manual*, and MCO P3500.19B, *Aviation Training and Readiness Manual, Volume V, Marine Air Command and Control System (MACCS) (Short title: T&R Manual, Volume V)*. NAVAIR 00-80T-114 ratings are issued by the FAA or designated examiners within the MATCD. Procedures for rating air traffic controller skills are outlined in applicable ICAO and FAA regulations. NAVAIR 00-80T-114 specifies the training and position requirements for controllers to progress through various levels of qualification within the tower or radar facility. All air traffic controllers in a deployment status are FAA certified for the qualified positions.

On-the-Job Training

Subsequent to basic ATC school training, each air traffic controller undergoes a period of on-the-job training (OJT) to attain hard-skill MOS and initial certifications. Technical MOS and proficiency training for tower and radar positions are conducted at Marine Corps ATC facilities. Approach controller training is available at Marine Corps Air Stations in Beaufort, Cherry Point, Iwakuni, and Yuma.

Follow-on Schools

Several formal and informal schools are available to air traffic controllers once initial certifications are achieved. Courses of instruction include—

- Weapons and Tactics Instructor.
- MMT Leaders Course (given by Marine Aviation Weapons and Tactics Squadron 1).
- Advanced Radar Air Traffic Control (Approach).
- Advanced MATCALS.
- Airspace Management.
- Terminal Instrument Procedures.
- Joint Air Tasking Order Process.
- Multi-TADIL Advanced Joint Interoperability.
- Joint Computer Applications.
- Airfield Management.

MATCD TECHNICIANS

MATCD technicians undergo their entry-level training at NAS, Pensacola. Maintenance technician training requirements are outlined in MCO P4790.12A, *Individual Training Standards System (Maintenance Training Management and Evaluation Program) (Short title: ITSS [MATMEP])*.

Training Levels

ITSS (MATMEP) training is—

- Conducted and maintained at the unit level.
- Task oriented and encompasses OJT for MATCALS equipment.
- Delineates four levels of certification:
  - Level 1, Apprentice Technician.
  - Level 2, Advanced Apprentice Technician.
  - Level 3, Journeyman Technician.
  - Level 4, Master Technician.

Follow-on Training

Marines demonstrating the required technical proficiency may be selected to attend advanced training. Two common follow-on schools available to technicians are the Microminiature Component Repair Course and the Maintenance Management Systems Analysis Course. Additional on-site training opportunities include the Operational Software Supplemental Training Course and system-specific, on-site technical training.

CREW AND INDIVIDUAL PROFICIENCY TRAINING

Training for individual MATCD crew members and the intercrew coordination is accomplished through several different methods, including both live and simulated training events. Two of the more common methods of attaining crew and individual proficiency is through ATC timeshare operations and simulated training.

ATC Timeshare Operations

Timeshare operations are operations conducted with tactical ATC equipment sited at existing air stations. They allow air traffic controllers assigned to air stations under the fleet assistance program to receive proficiency training on tactical equipment and to complete some training and readiness (T&R) manual training requirements. MATCD maintenance technicians and utilities personnel also receive training. Timeshare operations provide the local air station with backup FAA certified equipment in the event of station equipment failure.

Simulated Training

MATCALS has an internal simulation capability that allows for basic ground-controlled approach, flight data coordination, arrival control, and approach and departure control training. TADIL B data link training is accomplished via shelter-to-shelter simulation and live traffic data transfer.

Fleet Assistance Program

To maintain proficiency, Marine air traffic controllers in a garrison status are administratively assigned from their MATCD to

ATC duties at their local air station. Upon receipt of a deployment order for combat exercises or combat training, Marines return to their parent MATCDs for combat duty/training. This unique relationship provides for both ATC and tactical proficiency.

UNIT TRAINING

Unit training prepares the MATCD to perform its mission. Unit training can take on many forms, including command post exercises, simulated exercises, and field training exercises (FTXs). MATCD personnel are intimately involved in preparing training plans and coordinating with higher, adjacent, and subordinate air C2 and support elements.

Marine Aviation Planning Problem

Marine aviation planning problem (MAPP) exercises are low-cost, low-overhead training that allow commanders to train their staffs to perform special integration and control functions in a simulated environment. MAPP exercises are particularly effective for determining C2 requirements to support possible contingencies.

MACCS Integrated Simulated Training Exercise

The Marine integrated simulated training exercise is a MACG locally produced exercise that involves the detailed preparation of a simulated scenario and its subsequent execution at the MACCS level. It serves to prepare units for upcoming FTXs or contingencies.

Joint System Training Exercises

Similar to the integrated simulated training exercise, joint system training exercises (JSTEs) provide integrated systems training that incorporates the challenges of integrating the MACCS in the joint arena. JSTE scenarios have been developed to support joint training for probable contingency operations worldwide.

Field Training

Field training provides a unit with the most beneficial training opportunities available. Living and operating conditions are similar to those expected in combat. FTXs provide live operational training covering all phases of planning and operational employment including—

- Actual employment of an operational tactical approach control facility.
- Unique opportunity for training in an operational tactical control tower.
- Full liaison training with external ATC organizations.
- Full embark and planning training.
- Full maintenance support training.
- Integration training with MACCS agencies.

EVALUATION

Both individual and unit training must be continuously scrutinized and evaluated to identify areas for improvement. The two key instruments used to aid MACCS commanders in assessing their readiness are MCO P3500.19 and MCO 3501.9B.

APPENDIX E
GLOSSARY

Section I
Acronyms

AADC .... area air defense commander

ACA .... airspace control authority

ACE..aviation combat element

ACLS..automatic carrier landing system

ACO .... airspace control order

ACP..airspace control plan

ADCCN..............................air defense command and control net

ALS .... all-weather landing system

AM ....amplitude modulation

AO... area of operations

AOA .... amphibious objective area

ARFF... aircraft rescue and fire fighting

ASPARCS .... air surveillance and precision
approach radar control system

ATC ....air traffic control

ATCS... air traffic control subsystem

ATO ....air tasking order

BDZ.. base defense zone

C2 .... command and control

C3 ....command, control, and communications

CAC2S .... common aviation command and control system

CCS ....control and communications subsystem

CI/D .... combat information/detection

COA .... course of action

COMSEC.............................communications security

DASC ....direct air support center

DASC(A) ....direct air support center (airborne)

EMCON.. emission control

EP ....electronic protection

EW...electronic warfare

EW/C .... early warning/ control

FAA ....Federal Aviation Administration

FARP .... forward arming and refueling point

FM ....frequency modulation

FOB .... forward operating base

FTX .... field training exercise

HF...high frequency

HLZ .... helicopter landing zone

HMMWV .... high mobility multipurpose wheeled vehicle

HN .... host nation

H/O/X-TELL ....hand over/cross tell

Hz ....hertz

IADS .... integrated air defense system

ICAO ....International Civil Aviation Organization

IFF ....identification, friend or foe

IR... intelligence requirement
ITSS (MATMEP) .... Individual Training Standards System
(Maintenance Training Management
and Evaluation Program)

JP ....joint publication
JPALS........................... joint precision approach landing system
JSTE................................... joint system training exercise

kHz .... kilohertz

LAAD..low altitude air defense
LOS .... line of sight

MACCS .... Marine air command and control system
MACG ....Marine air control group
MACS .... Marine air control squadron
MAGTF .... Marine air-ground task force
MALS.....................................Marine aviation logistics squadron
MAPP..................................... Marine aviation planning problem
MATCALS ....Marine air traffic control and landing system
MATCD............................. Marine air traffic control detachment
MATMEP .... Maintenance Training Management
and Evaluation Program
MAWTS .... Marine aviation weapons and tactics squadron
MCCRES ..Marine Corps Combat Readiness Evaluation System
MCWP .... Marine Corps warfighting publication
MEF .... Marine expeditionary force
MEU(SOC) .... Marine expeditionary unit
(special operations capable)

MHz .... megahertz

MMT .... Marine air traffic control mobile team

MOS .... military occupational specialty

MRAALS .... Marine remote area approach
and landing system

MRR .... minimum-risk route

MUX .... multiplex

NAS .... naval air station

NATO .... North Atlantic Treaty Organization

NAVAIDS .... navigational aids

NAVAIR .... Naval Air Systems Command

NCOIC .... noncommissioned officer in charge

NEO .... noncombatant evacuation operation

nmi .... nautical mile

OOB .... order of battle

OJT .... on-the-job training

PDS .... processor display system

PFPS .... portable flight planning system

RADCON .... radiation control

RGR .... rapid ground refueling

RLST .... remote landing site tower

SAR .... search and rescue

SATCOM .... satellite communications

SCATANA..security control of air traffic and navigation aids

SHORAD ....short range air defense

SINCGARS..single-channel ground and airborne radio system

SNCO.. staff noncommissioned officer

SOP ....standing operating procedure

T&R .... training and readiness

TACAN ....tactical air navigation

TACC ....tactical air command center (USMC)

TADIL .... tactical digital information link

TAOC ....tactical air operations center

TATC.. tactical air traffic control

TCA ....terminal control area

TERP.. terminal instrument procedure

TLZ .... tactical landing zone

TSEC .... transmission security

TSN ....track supervision net

UAV.. unmanned aerial vehicle

UHF...ultrahigh frequency

VFR.. visual flight rules

VHF ....very high frequency

Section II
Definitions

air control—1. The authority to effect the maneuver of aircraft. The elements of air control are: air control agency, air controller, airspace control, operational control, positive control, procedural control, radar control, and terminal control. 2. The authority to direct the physical maneuver of aircraft in flight or to direct an aircraft or surface-to-air weapons (SAW) unit to engage a specific target. (Proposed for inclusion in MCRP 5-12C)

air controller—An individual especially trained for and assigned the duty of the control (by use of radio, radar, or other means) of such aircraft as may be allotted to him for operation within his area. (MCRP 5-12C)

air control agency—An organization possessing the capability to exercise air control. (MCRP 5-12C)

airspace control order—An order implementing the airspace control plan that provides the details of the approved requests for airspace control measures. It is published either as part of the air tasking order or as a separate document. Also called **ACO.** (JP 1-02)

airspace control plan—The document approved by the joint force commander that provides specific planning guidance and procedures for the airspace control system for the joint force area of responsibility and/or joint operations area. Also called **ACP.** (JP 1-02)

airspace management—The coordination, integration, and regulation of the use of airspace of defined dimensions. (JP 1-02)

area of operations—An operational area defined by the joint force commander for land and naval forces. Areas of operation do not typically encompass the entire operational area of the joint force commander, but should be large enough for component commanders to accomplish their missions and protect their forces. Also called **AO.** (JP 1-02)

area of responsibility—The geographical area associated with a combatant command within which a combatant commander has authority to plan and conduct operations. Also called **AOR.** (JP 1-02)

base defense zone—An air defense zone established around an air base and limited to the engagement envelope of short-range air defense weapons systems defending that base. Base defense zones have specific entry, exit, and identification, friend or foe procedures established. Also called **BDZ.** (JP 1-02)

emission control—The selective and controlled use of electromagnetic, acoustic, or other emitters to optimize command and control capabilities while minimizing, for operations security: a. detection by enemy sensors; b. mutual interference among friendly systems; and/or c. enemy interference with the ability to execute a military deception plan. Also called **EMCON.** (JP 1-02)

forward arming and refueling point—A temporary facility—organized, equipped, and deployed by an aviation commander, and normally located in the main battle area closer to the area where operations are being conducted than the aviation unit's combat service area—to provide fuel and ammunition necessary for the employment of aviation maneuver units in combat. The forward arming and refueling point permits combat aircraft to rapidly refuel and rearm simultaneously. Also called **FARP.** (JP 1-02)

forward operating base—An airfield used to support tactical operations without establishing full support facilities. The base may be used for an extended time period. Support by a main operating base will be required to provide backup support for a forward operating base. Also called **FOB.** (JP 1-02)

Marine air command and control system—A system that provides the aviation combat element commander with the means to command, coordinate, and control all air operations within an assigned sector and to coordinate air operations with other Services. It is composed of command and control agencies with communications-electronics equipment that incorporates a capability from manual through semiautomatic control. Also called **MACCS.** (JP 1-02)

Marine air traffic control mobile team—A task-organized element provided by the Marine air traffic control detachment that is trained and equipped to provide initial rapid response air traffic control, and command, control, and communications in support of MAGTF and joint missions. MMTs usually support operations at air sites, forward arming and refueling points, rapid ground refueling points, or lagger points. Normally, a fully manned and equipped mobile team capability can be provided on a 24-hour basis for up to 72 hours without resupply or augmentation. (Proposed for inclusion in MCRP 5-12C)

positive control—1. A method of airspace control that relies on positive identification, tracking, and direction of aircraft within an airspace, conducted with electronic means by an agency having the authority and responsibility therein. (JP 1-02) 2. The tactical control of aircraft by a designated control unit, whereby the aircraft receives orders affecting its movements which immediately transfer responsibility for the safe navigation of the aircraft to the unit issuing such orders. (MCRP 5-12C)

procedural control—A method of airspace control which relies on a combination of previously agreed and promulgated orders and procedures. (JP 1-02)

radar control—The operation of air traffic in a radar environment in which heading, altitude, and airspeed of the aircraft are directed by the control facility, and radar separation from other traffic is provided. (MCRP 5-12C)

sector—An area designated by boundaries within which a unit operates, and for which it is responsible. (JP 1-02, Part 1 of a 2-part definition)

terminal control—1. The authority to direct aircraft to maneuver into a position to deliver ordnance, passengers, or cargo to a specific location or target. Terminal control is a type of air control. 2. Any electronic, mechanical, or visual control given to aircraft to facilitate target acquisition and resolution. (JP 1-02)

terminal control area—A control area or portion thereof normally situated at the confluence of air traffic service routes in the vicinity of one or more major airfields. Also called **TCA**. (JP 1-02)

APPENDIX F
REFERENCES AND
RELATED PUBLICATIONS

Joint Publications (JPs)

0-2   Unified Action Armed Forces (UNAAF)

1-02   Department of Defense Dictionary of Military
                and Associated Terms

3-0   Doctrine for Joint Operations

3-02   Joint Doctrine for Amphibious Operations

3-02.1   Joint Doctrine for Landing Force Operations

3-52   Doctrine for Joint Airspace Control in
                the Combat Zone

3-54   Joint Doctrine for Operations Security

3-56.1   Command and Control for Joint Air Operations

Marine Corps Doctrinal Publication (MCDPs)

1   Warfighting

1-0   Marine Corps Operations

Marine Corps Warfighting Publications (MCWPs)

3-2   Aviation Operations

3-25   Control of Aircraft and Missiles

3-40.1   MAGTF Command and Control

5-11.1   MAGTF Aviation Planning

Marine Corps Reference Publications (MCRPs)

3-25A   Multi-Service Procedures for Joint Air Traffic Control

3-25F   Multi-Service Tactics, Techniques, and Procedures for Theater Air-Ground System

5-11.1A   MAGTF Aviation Planning Documents

5-12C   Marine Corps Supplement to the Department of Defense Dictionary of Military and Associated Terms

Marine Corps Orders (MCOs)

P3500.19B   Aviation Training and Readiness Manual, Volume V, Marine Air Command and Control System (MACCS) Short Title: T&R Manual, Volume V

3501.9B   Marine Corps Combat Readiness Evaluation System; Volume VIII; the Marine Air Command and Control System (MACCS)

P4790.12A   Individual Training Standards System (ITSS) (Maintenance, Training Management and Evaluation Program (Short Title: ITSS [MATMEP])

Miscellaneous

Naval Air Station Command (NAVAIR) 00-80T-114, Air Traffic Control Facilities Manual

www.ingramcontent.com/pod-product-compliance
Lightning Source LLC
Chambersburg PA
CBHW070552290526
45790CB00002B/652